THE CRUSADES CONTROVERSY

THE
CRUSADES
CONTROVERSY

Setting the Record Straight

THOMAS F. MADDEN

BEACON PUBLISHING
North Palm Beach, Florida

Portions of this text drawn from: Thomas F. Madden, *The Concise
History of the Crusades* (Rowman and Littlefield, 2013), by permission of
the publisher.

Design by Ashley Wirfel

ISBN: 978-1-63582-008-9 (softcover)
ISBN: 978-1-929266-13-5 (e-book)

Library of Congress Cataloging-in-Publication Data
Names: Madden, Thomas F., author.
Title: The crusades controversy : setting the record straight / Thomas
F. Madden.
Description: North Palm Beach : Beacon Publishing, 2017.
Identifiers: LCCN 2017025860 | ISBN 9781635820089 (softcover : alk.
paper) | ISBN 9781929266135 (e-book)
Subjects: LCSH: Crusades. | Crusades—Historiography. | Christianity
and other religions—Islam.
Classification: LCC D157 .M335 2017 | DDC
909.07—dc23

For more information on this title or other books and CDs available
through the Dynamic Catholic Book Program,
please visit www.DynamicCatholic.com.

The Dynamic Catholic Institute
5081 Olympic Blvd • Erlanger • Kentucky • 41018
Phone: 1–859–980–7900
Email: info@DynamicCatholic.com

First printing, August 2017

Printed in the United States of America

TABLE OF CONTENTS

PREFACE

✚

PRIOR TO SEPTEMBER 11, 2001, the world was a different place. Then, the Crusades were a faraway concept, an odd series of events in a distant and murky medieval past. Wars of religion seemed largely irrelevant to citizens of a modern secular civilization. That has changed. Terrorist attacks in the United States, Europe, and the Middle East continue to remind us all that there remain people in the world willing to kill or to be killed for their religion. Since then radical Muslims, known as Islamists, have continued to call on their coreligionists to take part in a worldwide jihad against the people of the West, whom the Islamists often refer to as "crusaders."

For their part, many in the West worry that their actions actually do resemble those of the medieval crusaders. American and European military forces, for example, remain stationed in the Middle East. And Israel, which enjoys significant Western support, is planted on soil that was once the medieval crusaders' kingdom. Western diplomats and politicians are careful to avoid any mention of the medieval Crusades around Muslim leaders, lest they appear insensitive or conjure up memories of the harm done by the medieval holy wars against them. Unfortunately, these sentiments and approaches are fueled on both sides by an extremely weak understanding of the actual Crusades or the medieval world in which they flourished. As a result, decisions—sometimes tragic decisions—are made based on deeply flawed concepts of history. By explaining just what the Crusades were and were not, this little book is an attempt to illuminate the complex relationship of the past to the present.

ONE

Are the Crusades to Blame?

I AM HAPPY TO OFFER my thoughts on something that is a bit of a rarity in my field of medieval history—a topic of timely interest. But that is precisely what the Crusades have become. Since the attacks of September 11, 2001, the Crusades have been pulled from the pages of history textbooks and spread across the front pages and television screens of America.

In 1999, I wrote one of those textbooks. It was a short introduction to a topic that was taught in only a few university classrooms around the country. Two years later, as Americans struggled to understand why they had been attacked, it left the classroom and began appearing on bookstore shelves nationwide. It remains there still. Because at the time I was the only living American scholar who had written a book on the Crusades, on September 12 I found my email inbox full and my phone ringing with requests for interviews. I was petrified when I did my first one—an NPR segment—but soon after they became routine. In the hundreds of interviews that I have given on the subject since then, the questions have frequently ended up at the same place: Are the Crusades the root cause of the struggle between Islam and the West? In other words, aren't the Crusades really to blame?

THE NEW CRUSADE

Osama bin Laden certainly thought so. He and his supporters never failed to describe the American war against terrorism as a new Crusade against Islam, and Americans themselves as crusaders. And this is not an uncommon view in the Middle East. The Islamic State of Iraq and Syria (ISIS), for example, routinely refers to the United States, Israel, and European nations as "crusader states." Ironically, this perspective on the medieval Crusades is actually not far from that of most people in the West. That is no coincidence, for, as I will argue, it is Western culture that provided Osama bin Laden and ISIS with a recovered memory of the Crusades.

OFFENSIVE ATTACK
OR DEFENSIVE REACTION?

In popular Western culture today, the Crusades are generally remembered as a series of holy wars against Islam led by power-hungry popes and fought by religious fanatics. They were the epitome of self-righteousness and intolerance, a black stain on the history of the Catholic Church in particular and Western civilization in general. A breed of proto-imperialists, the crusaders introduced Western aggression to the peaceful Middle East and then deformed the enlightened Muslim culture, leaving it in ruins. For variations on this theme one need not look far. See, for example, the 1995 BBC/A&E documentary, *The Crusades*, hosted by Terry Jones, or the 2005 History Channel documentary, or the 2005 epic Ridley Scott film, *The Kingdom of Heaven*. Indeed, I can think of no popular media portrayal of the Crusades that does not hold in some measure to this view.

Yet, that is not at all the way that Europeans viewed the Crusades when they were happening. Indeed, far from being an offensive attack on the lands of Islam,

Western Christians saw the Crusades as defensive reactions to Muslim aggression.

And they had a point. Christians in the eleventh century were not paranoid fanatics. Muslims really were gunning for them. From the time of Mohammed, the Muslim state had expanded by the sword. Traditional Muslim thought divided the world into two spheres, the Abode of Islam and the Abode of War. Christianity, and for that matter any other non-Muslim religion, has no abode. Christians and Jews can be tolerated within a Muslim state under Muslim rule. But their states must be destroyed and they must be conquered. When Mohammed was waging war against Mecca in the seventh century, Christianity was the dominant religion of power and wealth. As the faith of the Roman Empire, it spanned the entire Mediterranean, including the Middle East, where it was born. The Christian world, therefore, was a prime target for the earliest caliphs, and it would remain so for Muslim leaders for the next thousand years.

With enormous energy, the warriors of Islam struck out against the Christians shortly after Mohammed's death in 632. They were extremely successful. Palestine, Syria, Egypt—the most heavily Christian areas in the world—quickly succumbed. By the eighth century Muslim armies had conquered all of Christian North Africa and Spain. In the eleventh century the Seljuk Turks conquered Asia Minor (modern Turkey), which had been Christian since the days of St. Paul. The old Christian Roman Empire, known to modern historians as the Byzantine Empire, was reduced to little more than Greece. In desperation the emperor in Constantinople sent word to the Christians of western Europe asking them to aid their brothers and sisters in the East.

That is what gave birth to the Crusades. They were a response to more than four centuries of conquests in which Muslim armies had already captured two-thirds of the old Christian world. At some point Christianity as a faith and a culture either defended itself or was subsumed by Islam. The Crusades were that defense.

TWO

The Real Crusaders

POPE URBAN II CALLED the knights of Christendom to push back the conquests of Islam at the Council of Clermont in 1095. The response was tremendous. Many thousands of warriors took the vow of the cross and prepared for war. Why did they do it? The answer to that question has been badly misunderstood. It was once believed that crusaders were lacklands and ne'er-do-wells who took advantage of the situation to rob and pillage in a faraway land. Many high-school and college textbooks continue to present the crusaders in just this way.

However, during the past several decades computer-assisted charter studies have proven this to be wrong. Scholars have discovered that crusading knights were generally wealthy men with plenty of their own land in Europe. Nevertheless, they spent enormous sums to undertake their mission. Crusading was not cheap.

Even wealthy lords could easily impoverish themselves and their families by joining a Crusade. They did so not merely for material wealth (which they had already) but because they hoped to store up treasure where rust and moth could not corrupt. These were professional warriors who were keenly aware of the sinfulness of their profession and willing to undertake the hardships of the Crusade as a penitential act of charity and love.

Europe is littered with thousands of medieval charters attesting to these sentiments, in which these men and women still speak to us today. Of course, they were not opposed to capturing booty if it could be had. But the truth is that the Crusades were notoriously bad for plunder. A few people got rich, but the vast majority returned with nothing. Indeed many did not return at all. Approximately one out of two crusaders died on the journey.

THE REDEMPTION OF EASTERN CHRISTIANS

Urban II gave the crusaders two goals, both of which would remain central to the eastern Crusades for centuries. The first was to redeem the Christians of the East. As his successor, Pope Innocent III, later wrote:

> How does a man love according to divine precept his neighbor as himself when, knowing that his Christian brothers in faith and in name are held by the perfidious Muslims in strict confinement and weighed down by the yoke of heaviest servitude, he does not devote himself to the task of freeing them? . . . Is it, by chance, that you do not know that many thousands of Christians are bound in slavery and imprisoned by the Muslims, tortured with innumerable torments?

"Crusading," Jonathan Riley-Smith has rightly argued, was seen as "an act of love." In this case the love of one's neighbor. The Crusade was seen as an errand of mercy to right a terrible wrong. As the pope wrote to the Knights Templar, "you carry out in deeds the words of the Gospel, 'Greater love than this hath no man, that he lay down his life for his friends.'"

THE LIBERATION OF JERUSALEM

The second goal was the liberation of Jerusalem and the other places made holy by the life of Christ. The word *crusade* is modern. Medieval crusaders saw themselves as pilgrims to the Holy Sepulcher. The Crusade indulgence they received was canonically related to the pilgrimage indulgence. In medieval society it is not surprising that this goal was frequently described in feudal terms. When calling the Fifth Crusade in 1215, Innocent III wrote:

> Consider most dear sons, consider carefully that if any temporal king was thrown out of his domain and perhaps captured, would he not, when he was restored to his pristine liberty and the time had come for dispensing justice look on his vassals as unfaithful and traitors . . . unless they had committed not only their property but also their persons to the task of freeing him? . . . And similarly will not Jesus Christ, the king of kings and lord of lords, whose servant you cannot deny being, who joined your soul to your body, who redeemed you

with the Precious Blood . . . condemn you for the vice of ingratitude and the crime of infidelity if you neglect to help Him?

The re-conquest of Jerusalem, therefore, was understood by Christians as an act of restoration and an open declaration of one's love of God. Medieval people knew, of course, that God had the power to restore Jerusalem himself, indeed restore the whole world to his rule. Yet as St. Bernard of Clairvaux preached, he did not do so as a blessing to his people:

> Again I say, consider the Almighty's goodness and pay heed to His plans of mercy. He puts Himself under obligation to you, or rather feigns to do so, that He can help you to satisfy your obligations toward Himself. . . . I call blessed the generation that can seize an opportunity of such rich indulgence as this . . .

In medieval Europe, Crusades to the East were universally seen as acts of tremendous good. And how could they not? A crusader was one who, at great expense and personal peril, sought to rescue the downtrodden, defend the defenseless, and restore to Christendom what had been violently taken away. A Crusade indulgence, then, was a formal recognition of the penitential component of these actions. Crusaders were sinners. They undertook the Crusade not only to defend their world, but to atone for their sins. By the nature of their profession, warriors put their souls at risk. The Crusade was a means for them to save their souls. And that was no small thing. In the medieval world, where death was always near at hand, the salvation of one's soul meant everything. It was a matter of constant concern.

THREE

The First Crusade: A Lone Success

BY ANY RECKONING the First Crusade was a long shot. There was no leader, no chain of command, no supply lines, no detailed strategy. It was simply thousands of warriors marching deep into enemy territory, committed to a common cause. Many of them died, either in battle or through disease or starvation. It was a rough campaign, one that seemed always on the brink of disaster. Yet it was astonishingly successful. By 1098 the crusaders had restored Nicaea and Antioch to Christian rule. In July 1099 they conquered Jerusalem and began to build a Christian state in Palestine. The joy in Europe was unbridled. It seemed that the tide of history, which had lifted the Muslims to such heights, was at last turning.

But it was not. When we think about the Middle Ages it is easy to view Europe in light of what it became, rather than what it was. The colossus of the medieval world was Islam, not Christendom. The Crusades are interesting because they were an attempt to counter that trend. But in five centuries of crusading, it was only the First Crusade that significantly rolled back the military progress of Islam in the East. It was all downhill from there. Once the Muslim states in the region unified against the Kingdom of Jerusalem, it was doomed.

THE FAILURE OF THE CRUSADES

If the Crusades represented the highest good, how could they fail? If crusaders fought for God, why did the victories go to his enemies? These were questions that vexed Christians in the Middle Ages. The answer lay no further than the Bible. The ancient Israelites, God's chosen people, had frequently been defeated by other godless people. It was not because God had abandoned them, or because he favored the foreigners. Instead, he used these defeats as a means of chastising his people for their sins. Europeans took their defeats at the hands of Muslims as clear evidence of their sinfulness. This led to renewed attempts to purify the Church and Christian society throughout the Middle Ages. Success in the Crusades became the barometer of the soul of Christendom. When they succeeded, God was once again pleased with his people. The problem was, they did not succeed.

The last Christian outpost in the Holy Land fell in 1291. In subsequent centuries the dramatic growth of Muslim power, particularly under the Ottoman Empire, spelled only further defeats for the West. By the fourteenth century the Crusades were no longer wars to turn back Muslim conquests in faraway lands, but desperate and largely unsuccessful attempts to defend Europe itself against Muslim invasion. By the sixteenth century the Ottoman Turks had conquered all of the Middle East, North Africa, and southeastern Europe, including areas today that are Greece, Bulgaria, Albania, Hungary, and others. Sultan Suleiman the Magnificent came within a hair's breadth of conquering Vienna, which would have left all of Germany at his mercy. Vienna was saved by freak rain storms, not the Crusades.

REASONS FOR THE COLLAPSE

It was in the sixteenth century, when western Europe was in the gravest danger of Muslim conquest, that the

Crusades as an institution began to collapse utterly. There were many reasons for this. As secular authority in Europe increased, religious unity crumbled. Europeans began dividing themselves along political lines. In addition, there was a strong desire in the West for church reform. Reformers invariably criticized doctrines central to crusading, in particular the secular authority of the pope and the doctrine of indulgence. With the spread of the Protestant Reformation crusading was viewed along confessional lines. Protestants like Martin Luther condemned the Crusades as the tool of a corrupt papacy. Yet even Protestants had to reckon with the awesome power of the Turks and the danger it posed to Christian Europe. If the Crusades were morally bankrupt, as the Protestants insisted, how then could Europeans unite to defend against the common enemy?

For a thousand years after the death of the prophet Mohammed, Muslim armies had managed to conquer fully three quarters of the old Christian world, despite the efforts of generations of crusaders to halt or turn back the advance. An impartial observer at the time might well have concluded that Christendom was a doomed remnant of the ancient Roman Empire, destined to be supplanted by the more youthful and energetic religion and culture of Islam. Yet that observer would have been wrong. Within Europe new ideas were brewing that would have dramatic and unprecedented repercussions, not just in the Mediterranean, but across the entire world. Born out of a unique blend of faith, reason, individualism, and entrepreneurialism, those ideas produced a rapid increase in scientific experimentation with immediately practical applications. By the seventeenth century European wealth and power was growing exponentially. Europeans were entering a new and unprecedented age.

FOUR

A New Age

IT IS ONE OF THE MOST remarkable events in history that the Christian West, an internally divided region seemingly on the brink of conquest by a powerful empire, suddenly burst forth with amazing new energy, neutralizing its enemies and expanding across the globe. The specter of advancing Muslim armies, which for centuries had posed such danger to the Christian West, no longer constituted a serious threat. Indeed, as the gaze of Europeans spanned new global horizons, they soon forgot that such a threat had existed at all. The Muslim world was no longer viewed as a dreaded enemy, but simply one more backward culture. From that perspective the medieval Crusades began to seem distant and unnecessary—a discarded artifact from the childhood of a civilization.

THE ENLIGHTENMENT VIEW

The eighteenth century saw the rise of the Enlightenment with its strict emphasis on rational thought, religious tolerance, and anticlericalism. In an intellectual atmosphere like that the medieval Crusades did not fare well. Enlightenment historians such as Voltaire and Edward Gibbon viewed the Middle Ages as a pool of ignorance, superstition, and fanaticism that stood between them and the glories of antiquity. Not surprisingly, the Crusades were described as a bizarre manifestation of medieval barbarism in which thousands of the deceived and the foolish marched through rivers of blood in a pitiful attempt to save their souls. In his famous *Decline and Fall of the Roman Empire* (1776–88), Edward Gibbon insisted that nothing good at all came out of the Crusades, except perhaps Europe's exposure to more sophisticated Eastern cultures.

THE ROMANTIC IDEOLOGY

During the nineteenth century the Crusades were rehabilitated by the Romantic movement, which adored everything medieval, and by the new ideologies of nationalism and imperialism. French nationalists, for example, saw their country as both the cultural epicenter and the natural leader of Europe. They proudly looked back on the medieval Crusades, born and nurtured in medieval France, as a clear example of their country's greatness. When the French invaded and conquered Algeria in 1830 the campaign was widely described as a successor to St. Louis IX's Crusade to Tunisia in 1270. However, the Crusades were refashioned to become something that they never were—France's first attempt to bring the fruits of Western civilization to the Muslim world. As such, the new and improved Crusades were retooled to become the first chapter in European colonialism.

This worked well, since all European colonial powers could boast famous crusaders in their histories. Germany had Frederick Barbarossa, England had Richard the Lionheart, and even tiny Belgium had Godfrey de Bouillon.

The aftermath of World War I brought about the fall of the once-mighty Ottoman Empire, the last great Muslim state. In dividing up the remains the League of Nations gave control of Palestine and Syria to Britain and France. Steeped in these imagined medieval precedents, Europeans could scarcely have avoided seeing this colonialism as the final chapter in the long history of the Crusades.

The popular London magazine, *Punch*, ran a drawing of Richard the Lionheart watching the British entry into Jerusalem with the caption, "At last, my dream come true." After taking command in Syria, the French General Henri Gouraud remarked, "Behold, Saladin, we have returned."[1]

---

[1] Jonathan Riley-Smith, "Islam and the Crusades in History and Imagination, 8 November 1898–11 September 2001," *Crusades* 2 (2003), p. 158.

FIVE

The Muslim Memory

IT IS COMMONLY SAID that memories in the Middle East are long, that although the Crusades may have been forgotten in the West, they are still vividly remembered where they happened. For example, in a speech delivered at Georgetown University a few weeks after the 9/11 attacks, former President Bill Clinton stated:

> Those of us who come from various European lineages are not blameless. Indeed, in the First Crusade, when the Christian soldiers took Jerusalem, they first burned a synagogue with three hundred Jews in it, and proceeded to kill every woman and child who was Muslim on the Temple Mount. The contemporaneous descriptions of the event describe soldiers walking on the Temple Mount, a holy place to Christians, with blood running up

to their knees. I can tell you that that story is still being told today in the Middle East, and we are still paying for it.

Clinton is correct that the story is still told, but it is neither accurate nor is it a long-held memory of a traumatic event. Indeed, the simple and startling fact is that the Crusades were virtually unknown in the Muslim world even a century ago. The term for the Crusades, *harb al-salib*, was only introduced into the Arab language in the mid-nineteenth century. The first Arabic history of the Crusades was not written until 1899. In other words, one hundred or so years ago no one at all in the Middle East was telling the president's story.

How is that possible? How could Muslims not remember centuries of Christian holy wars waged against them? It must be remembered that although the Crusades were of monumental importance to Europeans, they were a very minor, largely insignificant thing to the vast Muslim world. Traditionally, Muslims took very little interest in people or events outside of the *dar al-Islam*. There was, therefore, nothing to differentiate the Crusades from any other of the numerous and nearly constant wars fought against infidels.

The Crusades were, in any case, unsuccessful and thus irrelevant. A Western traveler in the eighteenth century would have been hard pressed to find a Muslim in the Middle East who had heard of the Crusades. Even in the nineteenth century they were known only to a handful of intellectuals. In the grand sweep of Islamic history the Crusades simply did not matter.

RESCUED FROM OBSCURITY

Muslim perceptions of their own history changed in the twentieth century. Rescued from obscurity, the Crusades were discovered and given a place of importance that they had never enjoyed before. The "long memory" of the Crusades in the Muslim world is, in fact, a constructed memory—one in which the memory is much younger than the event itself. How did this come about? As we have seen, when European colonial powers took control of the Middle East in the wake of the collapse of the Ottoman Empire, they brought with them a concept of the Crusades and an understanding of their own actions within that medieval context. In books and colonial schools Europeans taught the Muslim world about the Crusades. They were vividly described as heroic enterprises whose aim, like that of the Europeans, was to bring civilization to the Middle East.

THE SULTAN SALADIN

It was also at this time that Saladin was reintroduced to the Muslim world. Hard as it may be to believe, the famous sultan had been virtually forgotten in the Middle East. On further reflection, though, that should not be too surprising. Saladin was a Kurd, an ethnic group not well liked by either Arabs or Turks. Although he had won the Battle of Hattin in 1187 and subsequently conquered Jerusalem and much of the crusader kingdom, Saladin's successes as well as his dynasty were short-lived. The Third Crusade managed to erase most of his conquests. Even Jerusalem would not remain permanently in Muslim hands.

Saladin may have been forgotten in the Middle East, but he was very well remembered in western Europe. In part, this was because his manners and actions seemed to have much in common with a chivalric knight. There is no doubt that Richard the Lionheart thought highly of Saladin. This made him a perfect foil for the celebrated crusader king, and he therefore figured prominently in medieval romances.

In time, Western storytellers would have Saladin being knighted and even secretly converting to Christianity. In medieval Venice the name *Saladin* had a brief period of popularity for Christian boys. It was this idealized Saladin—the noble warrior, merciful ruler, and great unifier—that modern Europeans brought with them when they returned to the Middle East. This occurred most dramatically in 1899 when Kaiser Wilhelm II of Germany visited the neglected and largely forgotten tomb of Saladin in Damascus. Shocked at the poor state of the monument, Wilhelm paid for the creation of a new mausoleum on which he placed a bronze wreath with the inscription, "From one great emperor to another."

NATIONALISTS AND ISLAMISTS

Two main groups, nationalists and Islamists, stood in opposition to European colonialism in the Middle East in the twentieth century. Nationalists demanded sovereign states independent of European rule. Islamists looked to the Koran and Islamic history, insisting that Muslims must renew the jihad and restore the unity of the *dar al-Islam*. Nationalists and Islamists were naturally antagonistic to each other, yet they both shared a common desire to eject European powers from the Middle East. Since the colonialists had themselves equated their occupation with the medieval Crusades, it was natural enough for Muslims, and especially Arabs, to do the same. This became particularly pronounced after the creation of the state of Israel, which Arabs contended was a new crusader kingdom. The fact that Israel was Jewish was irrelevant. It was still a non-Muslim state planted in the former lands of the crusaders.

THE LEGACY OF IMPERIALISM

By the 1950s colonialism was largely discredited in the West. In the United States and Britain intellectuals began to calculate the harm done to the world by the "legacy of imperialism." The Crusades, which had already been redefined as the West's first colonial venture, were tarred with the same brush. They were, it was argued, nothing more than destructive wars of greed cynically covered in a thin veneer of pious platitudes.

Indeed, so great was this feeling, primarily among Western elites and intellectuals, that a large number of them took part in a walk in the footsteps of the First Crusade on its 900th anniversary in 1999. The purpose of the Reconciliation Walk was to apologize to everyone in the Middle East for the Crusades and their continued legacy. The text of the written apology which was delivered by the thousands read:

> Nine hundred years ago, our forefathers carried the name of Jesus Christ in battle across the Middle East. Fuelled by fear, greed, and hatred, they betrayed the name of Christ . . . We deeply regret the atrocities committed in the name of Christ. . . . Where they were motivated by hatred and prejudice, we offer love and brotherhood.

GOOD VERSUS EVIL

Arab nationalists and Islamists agreed fully with this interpretation of the Crusades. Poverty, corruption, and violence in the Middle East were said to be the lingering effects of the Crusades and subsequent European imperialism. The Muslim world had failed to keep up with the West because it had been dealt a debilitating blow by the crusaders, a blow that was repeated by their European descendents in the nineteenth century. The dictators that ruled the now-independent Arab states seized on this as a means of deflecting criticism of their own regimes. Generations of Arab schoolchildren have been taught that the Crusades were a clear case of good versus evil. Rapacious and zealous crusaders swept into a peaceful and sophisticated Muslim world leaving carnage and destruction in their wake. Yet Saladin, the great and heroic leader, led the Muslims to victory, capturing Jerusalem and defeating the invaders.

Not surprisingly, Arab leaders today continue to invoke this recovered memory of Saladin. In 1992, the Syrian leader Hafez Asad placed a life-size equestrian statue of the sultan, complete with defeated crusader lords groveling below, directly in front of the Damascus citadel not a hundred yards away from a massive portrait of Asad himself. A depiction of the statue even appears on the Syrian currency. Former President of

Iraq, Saddam Hussein, regularly referred to himself as a new Saladin who would unite the Arab world against their common foes (even though Saladin was no Arab).

SIX

Today's Struggle between Islamists
and the West

TODAY MANY ISLAMISTS BELIEVE that the West, and in particular the United States, is promoting a new Crusade, one that is being fought on many fronts. American military bases, especially those in Muslim countries, are described as the return of crusader forces. When Osama bin Laden issued his Declaration of Jihad on February 23, 1998, he did so against the "Jews and crusaders." He wrote, "The Arabian Peninsula has never—since Allah made it flat, created its desert, and encircled it with seas—been stormed by any forces like the crusader armies spreading in it like locusts."

The attacks on the United States on September 11, 2001, were viewed by Islamists as an act of jihad against a crusading state. They were a new Battle of Hattin, a new Field of Blood. When the United States declared war on Afghanistan and Islamist terrorism, European countries rose up in support. This, too, Islamists viewed through the prism of the Crusades. In an October 2001 al-Jazeera interview bin Laden remarked, "This is a recurring war. The original Crusades were brought by Richard from Britain, Louis from France, and Barbarossa from Germany. Today the crusading countries rushed as soon as Bush raised the cross. They accepted the rule of the cross."

In Amin Maalouf's popular book, *The Crusades through Arab Eyes*, he asks the question, "Can we go so far as to claim that the Crusades marked the beginning of the rise of Western Europe—which would gradually come to dominate the world—and sounded the death knell of Arab civilization?" With some qualification he answers in the affirmative. "Although the epoch of the Crusades ignited a genuine economic and cultural revolution in western Europe, in the Orient these holy wars led to long centuries of decadence and obscurantism. Assaulted from all quarters, the Muslim world turned in on itself." He goes on, "There can be no doubt that the schism between these two worlds dates from the Crusades, deeply felt by the Arabs, even today, as an act of rape."[2]

Maalouf, who is a novelist, offers a conclusion that is perfectly in keeping with the modern popular consensus in both the Middle East and the West. Popular it may be, yet it is nonetheless wrong. Scholars have long argued that the Crusades had no beneficial effect on Europe's economy. Indeed, they constituted a massive drain on resources. The rise of population and wealth in Europe predated the Crusades, indeed allowed them to happen at all. Rather than decadent or "assaulted on all sides" the Muslim world was growing to ever new heights of power and prosperity long after the destruction of the crusader states in 1291.

It was the Muslim world, under the rule of the Ottoman sultans, that would invade western Europe, seriously threatening the survival of the last remnant of Christendom. The Crusades contributed nothing to the decline of the Muslim world. Indeed, they are evidence

[2] Amin Maalouf, *The Crusades Through Arab Eyes*, trans. Jon Rothschild (New York: Schocken, 1984), pp. 261, 264, 266.

of the decline of the Christian West, which was forced to mount these desperate expeditions to defend against ever-expanding Muslim empires.

ARE THE CRUSADES TO BLAME?

Returning to the question at the beginning of chapter one—"Are the Crusades to blame for the current tensions between Islam and the West?"—the simple answer is no. The Crusades were a medieval phenomenon, a part of a medieval world that is very different from our world today. Christians saw the Crusades to the east as religious wars waged in defense of Christendom. For their part, medieval Muslims had no understanding or interest in the Crusades. The crusader kingdom of Jerusalem was simply one more state in an already chaotic political landscape. When the Muslims of the region finally united, they dispatched the infidels and that was all. They were a tiny crumb in the big soup of Islamic history.

It is not the Crusades that led to the attacks of September 11, but an artificial memory of the Crusades constructed by modern colonial powers and passed down by Arab nationalists and Islamists. This new memory strips the medieval expeditions of every aspect of their age, dressing them up instead in the tattered rags of nineteenth-century imperialism. The Crusades have thus become an icon for modern agendas that medieval Christians and Muslims could scarcely have understood, let alone condoned.

ABOUT THE AUTHOR

Thomas F. Madden is professor of medieval history and director of the Center for Medieval and Renaissance Studies at Saint Louis University. A recognized expert on the Crusades, he has appeared in such venues as National Public Radio, PBS, and the *New York Times*. His publications include *Crusades: The Illustrated History*; *The Fourth Crusade: The Conquest of Constantinople*; *Venice: A New History*; *Istanbul: City of Majesty at the Crossroads of the World*; and *The Concise History of the Crusades*.

THE
DYNAMIC CATHOLIC
INSTITUTE

[MISSION]

To re-energize the Catholic Church in America by
developing world-class resources that inspire people to
rediscover the genius of Catholicism.

[VISION]

To be the innovative leader in the New Evangelization
helping Catholics and their parishes become
the-best-version-of-themselves.

Join us in re-energizing the Catholic Church.
Become a Dynamic Catholic Ambassador today!

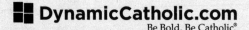

DynamicCatholic.com
Be Bold. Be Catholic.®